SĀKET

An English Transcreation
(Inspired by the Hindi Epic Sākēt of Maithili Sharan Gupt)

A Miltonic–Tagorian Devotional Epic

by

Anand Kumar Ashodhiya

(Self-published under the imprint "Avikavani Publishers")
First Edition : 2025

"Where Duty became Love,
and Love became Dharma."

Avikavani Publishers, Shahpur Turk, Sonipat, Haryana, 2025

SĀKET

An English Transcreation
(Inspired by the Hindi Epic Sākēt of Maithili Sharan Gupt)
A Miltonic–Tagorian Devotional Epic
by
Anand Kumar Ashodhiya

Published by
Avikavani Publishers
(Self-publishing imprint of **Anand Kumar Ashodhiya**)
Shahpur Turk, Sonipat, Haryana, India
ISBN: 978-93-5469-845-3
First Edition : 2025

Presented By:
Anand Kumar Ashodhiya
for Avikavani Publishers

IMPRINT & COPYRIGHT PAGE

Title: *SĀKET: An English Transcreation (Inspired by the Hindi Epic Sākēt of Maithili Sharan Gupt)*

A Miltonic–Tagorian Devotional Epic
by
Anand Kumar Ashodhiya

Legal Public-Domain Declaration (for SĀKET)

Legal Status of Source Text:

The original Hindi epic *Sākēt* by **Maithili Sharan Gupt (1886–1964)** is confirmed to be in the **Public Domain in India**, pursuant to **Section 22 of the Indian Copyright Act, 1957**, which provides protection for sixty years after the author's death. As this term expired on **31 December 2024**, *Sākēt* entered the public domain effective **1 January 2025**.

Any quotations from the Hindi text are reproduced solely for **scholarly and literary reference** under the principle of fair use.

First Edition, 2025

Published worldwide under the independent literary imprint **AVIKAVANI PUBLISHERS**
(An Imprint of Anand Kumar Ashodhiya)

Original Hindi Text: *Sākēt* by Maithili Sharan Gupt — Public Domain (India)

ISBN: 978-93-5469-845-3

LEGAL & PUBLISHING NOTES

Title: *SĀKET: An English Transcreation (Inspired by the Hindi Epic Sākēt of Maithili Sharan Gupt)*

A Miltonic–Tagorian Devotional Epic
by

Anand Kumar Ashodhiya

Author / Transcreator: Anand Kumar Ashodhiya
Year of Publication: 2025

Copyright & Rights Statement

Edition Information

First Edition (Scholarly Transcreation Format)
All citations correspond to standard Hindi editions of *Sākēt* published by Lokbharti Prakashan, Sahitya Akademi, and Gita Press, Gorakhpur.

ISBN: 978-93-5469-845-3

Disclaimer

This book is a creative transcreation, not a literal translation.
While rooted in Maithili Sharan Gupt's original vision, it re-imagines *Sākēt* in an English epic idiom (Miltonic–Tagorian style) to convey its *dharmic*, moral, and emotional essence to a global audience.

Publication and Design Credits
Cover Art and Interior Design © Avikavani Publishers, 2025

Published by **Avikavani Publishers**
(An Independent Literary Imprint of Anand Kumar Ashodhiya)

Legal Notice

Legal Public-Domain Declaration (for SĀKET)

Legal Status of Source Text: The original Hindi epic *Sākēt* by **Maithili Sharan Gupt (1886–1964)** is confirmed to be in the **Public Domain in India**, pursuant to **Section 22 of the Indian Copyright Act, 1957**, which provides protection for sixty years after the author's death. As this term expired on **31 December 2024**, *Sākēt* entered the public domain effective **1 January 2025**.

This English poetic adaptation (*SĀKET — An English Transcreation*) is an **independent creative work** based on the public-domain text and constitutes a new and original literary composition © **Anand Kumar Ashodhiya, 2025**.

Any quotations from the Hindi text are reproduced solely for **scholarly and literary reference** under the principle of fair use.

Dedication

To my Gurudev,
Śrī Paleram Dahiya Halālpuriyā Ji
(Custodian of the Ragni Tradition)

whose voice still resounds in my verses—
a living echo of the soil and the spirit.

To him, I owe the discipline of melody,
the faith in the word,
and the courage to carry the torch of Lok–Sanskriti
into the quiet dawn of modern song.

This book is an offering of remembrance and reverence.

— **Anand Kumar Ashodhiya**
Transcreator of SĀKET
Avikavani Publishers, 2025

Epigraph

"अयि दयामयि देवि, सुखदे, सारदे,
इधर भी निज वरद-पाणि पसार दे।
दास की यह देह-तन्त्री सार दे,
रोम-तारों में नई झंकार दे॥"
— Maithili Sharan Gupt, Sākēt (I.1)

Transcreation (English rendering):

O merciful Goddess, giver of joy, Saraswati divine,
stretch forth Thy boon-bestowing hand even here.
Tune this frail instrument of flesh anew,
and let each trembling nerve resound with living song.

"चल अयोध्या के लिए, सज साज तू,
माँ, मुझे कृतकृत्य कर दे आज तू॥"
— Sākēt (I.1)

Transcreation (English rendering):

Prepare, O Mother, for the journey to Ayodhya—
make me worthy of this sacred path;
let this day fulfill the vow of my being.

(These opening verses, drawn from the first Sarga of Sākēt, *form the spiritual overture of the entire work — invoking both the Muse of speech and the sanctity of purpose.)*

Epigraph Commentary

"Where poetry becomes prayer, and art becomes dharma —
there begins the pilgrim's song of Ayodhya."

In these opening invocations, *Gupt* places his soul before the eternal Muse — not merely as a poet seeking eloquence, but as a pilgrim yearning for consecration. Saraswati, the embodiment of divine speech, is entreated to awaken the inner music of the human frame, to turn each nerve and vein into a vibrating string of devotion. The act of creation here is not an assertion of self, but a surrender of selfhood — the poet becomes the instrument through which the cosmic harmony resounds.

The call *"चल अयोध्या के लिए, सज साज तू"* ("Prepare for the journey to Ayodhya") extends beyond geography; it is a summons of the spirit. Ayodhya, the city of Rama, stands not only as a locus of dharma and beauty, but as the symbol of inner order, the regained harmony of the human soul. The poet prays not for inspiration alone, but for *worthiness* — that his work may be an offering rather than an achievement, a sādhanā rather than an ornament.

This twofold invocation thus sanctifies both art and aspiration. It declares that the pilgrimage of poetry is inseparable from the pilgrimage of life — that speech, when purified by love and discipline, becomes a bridge between the mortal and the divine. As in *Milton's* "Sing, Heavenly Muse," and *Tagore's* "Let my life be music to Thee," here too the word is worship, and creation itself a form of prayer.

FOREWORD

On Maithili Sharan Gupt and the Eternal Voice of Sākēt
By K. Lal
(Krishna Lal, Retired Lecturer in English, Rohtak, Haryana)

There are ages in human history when poetry becomes a vessel of revelation—when the word, sanctified by truth, is not merely art, but a pilgrimage. Such was the age of Maithili Sharan Gupt, and such is his immortal testament, *Sākēt*.

When *Sākēt* first appeared in the early twentieth century, India stood poised between the twilight of bondage and the dawn of self-realization. It was a time when the spiritual nerve of a civilization long suppressed sought once again to express itself—not through violence, but through remembrance. Gupt, in his quiet, luminous way, gave voice to that remembrance.

He returned to the ancient story of Rama—not to re-tell an epic of divine triumph, but to reimagine its inner music. In *Sākēt,* Ayodhya is no longer merely a city of kings; it becomes the emblem of a moral universe, where dharma, sacrifice, and compassion converge. Rama is not the remote god of ritual reverence, but the ideal of ethical manhood, whose suffering redeems humanity itself. Sita, too, is no longer a shadowed consort; she is the luminous heart of endurance, the silent conscience of civilization.

Gupt's genius lay in transfiguring legend into living philosophy. His verse carries the cadence of the *Ramayana* yet speaks with the tenderness of the human soul. In his language, the Sanskritic grandeur of Valmiki meets the inward lyricism of Kabir and the moral clarity of Gandhi. The result is a poetry that is both epic and intimate, both national and universal.

To read *Sākēt* is to stand at the confluence of history and eternity. Through its measured rhythm and serene moral vision, we are invited to contemplate not the politics of empire, but the governance of the self; not conquest, but conscience. The Ayodhya that Gupt envisions is not a geographic place—it is a condition of the soul, a state of harmony where power serves love and love sanctifies duty.

This English adaptation, though written in another tongue, aspires to carry that same inner resonance. It does not merely transcreate the outer form of Gupt's verse; it seeks to convey the pulse of his faith—the rhythm of the eternal Indian consciousness that perceives the divine not as abstraction, but as relationship: the dialogue between Rama and Sita, between renunciation and compassion, between humanity and the Infinite.

Gupt once said that poetry is the sacred duty of awakening—of reminding man of his forgotten nobility. In that spirit, *Sākēt* is more than a work of literature; it is a scripture of the heart. To render it anew for English readers is to participate in that same act of remembrance—to proclaim that dharma, as Gupt understood it, is not bound to one age or one people, but is the perennial rhythm of Truth itself.

May this English *Sākēt* speak not only to scholars, but to all who seek beauty without vanity, devotion without dogma, and strength without cruelty. For the light of Ayodhya, once kindled in Gupt's verse, still shines wherever men and women strive to live in harmony with the eternal law of love.

— K. Lal
(Krishna Lal, Retired Lecturer in English)
Rohtak, Haryana – 2025

PREFACE

By Dr. Purnmal Gaur
(Former Director, Haryana Sahitya Academy, Panchkula, Government of Haryana)

"Every civilization dreams its truth in verse."

When Maithili Sharan Gupt wrote *Sākēt*, he rekindled the moral consciousness of a nation in transition. His poetry did not merely narrate the story of Rāma; it rediscovered the eternal covenant between *Dharma* and humanity. In *Sākēt*, Ayodhya ceases to be a geographical city and becomes a state of inner equilibrium — where righteousness is not ritual, but compassion made luminous through action. Few modern poets have given to India such a synthesis of faith and reason, restraint and radiance.

In *SĀKET — An English Transcreation*, Anand Kumar Ashodhiya re-imagines that same spiritual geography for the modern, English-speaking world. His work does not attempt to translate Gupt's words but to transmute their essence. The language of English becomes here not a vessel of exile, but of return — a renewed medium for the moral music of Ayodhya. The result is a work that unites the majesty of Miltonic blank verse with the tenderness of Tagorean introspection. It speaks with reverence, yet with creative independence, allowing Gupt's humanism to resonate through a global idiom.

Gupt's vision was that of a poet-saint who saw divinity reflected in disciplined humanity. His *Maryādā Puruṣottam* is no remote deity but the exemplar of ethical will; his Sītā, no shadowed consort but the embodiment of luminous endurance. Ashodhiya's transcreation preserves this human core. His diction is austere yet musical; his imagery steeped in Sanskritic symbolism yet free of ornamentation. To read these cantos is to hear again the timeless cadence of the Indian conscience — a poetry where love matures into duty and duty ripens into peace.

To attempt Sākēt in another tongue is not to repeat it, but to remember it anew. Through this work, poetry becomes prayer in translation — not imitation, but participation in the sacred labour of renewal. It restores to the English epic the moral gravity of the Indian heart and reminds us that the voice of Ayodhya still calls across languages and ages.

— Dr. Puranmal Gaur
(Former Director, Haryana Sahitya Academy, Panchkula, Government of Haryana)

TRANSCREATOR'S NOTE

To "translate" *Sākēt* would be to diminish its secret light; to *transcreate* it is to serve that light in another form. The power of Gupt's poetry lies not in narrative but in *bhāva* — that subtle harmony of devotion, discipline, and moral radiance that breathes through every verse. This English rendering, therefore, does not attempt line-for-line correspondence. It is a poetic re-enactment: an attempt to let the voice of Ayodhya speak once more in the rhythm of another world.

The verse form follows the Miltonic cadence — majestic, reflective, sonorous — interwoven with Tagorean lyricism and Vedic symbolism. Its diction seeks elevation without estrangement: a language at once sacred and accessible, touched with Sanskritic echoes — *the forest of prayer, the lamp of compassion, the chariot of renunciation.* Each canto mirrors the ethical and emotional curve of Gupt's original but flows as an independent English epic. The aim is fidelity of spirit, not of syllable.

NOTE ON THE LITERARY STATUS OF THIS TRANSCREATION

This work belongs to the evolving genre of *transcreation* — an interpretive re-imagining that stands between translation and original composition. Its purpose is to transmit the ethical resonance, spiritual beauty, and human tenderness that form the living pulse of Gupt's *Sākēt*. In this sense, it follows the creative lineage of Tagore's *Gitanjali* in English, A. K. Ramanujan's interpretive translations, and Ezra Pound's *Cathay* — works that reach poetic truth through creative re-birth rather than literal replication.

In the act of transcreation, language becomes a consecrated space for the re-incarnation of meaning. The transcreator listens to the inner rhythm of the source text and then composes anew in a voice native to another linguistic world. *SĀKET — An English Transcreation* thus stands beside Gupt's *Sākēt* not as its echo, but as its mirror — faithful in devotion, free in expression, and luminous with the same moral flame that once illumined Ayodhya.

INTRODUCTION: THE WORLD OF *SĀKĒT*

Rashtrakavi Maithili Sharan Gupt (1886–1964)

The original author of the Hindi epic *Sākēt* (1932), who pioneered the use of *Khari Boli* (modern vernacular Hindi) in epic poetry. Gupt connected the *Ramkatha* to modern concepts of national consciousness, humanism, and domestic *dharma*.

Image Source: Public Domain

Gupt and the Rise of the Modern Hindi Epic

I. The Ethos of Ayodhya — Dharma, Compassion, Duty

In the moral imagination of India, *Ayodhya* is not a city merely built of stone and sovereignty; it is a spiritual archetype, a mirror of order (*rta*) where justice, tenderness, and truth cohere into a single light. In the early twentieth century—an age when India was rediscovering her ethical voice amid colonial disquiet—Maithili Sharan Gupt restored this archetype to consciousness through his epic poem *Sākēt*.

For Gupt, *Ayodhya* is less geography than *state of being*. It is the realized form of dharma—an equilibrium between outer governance and inward grace. Rama's reign embodies law without tyranny; Sita's presence lends that law its living compassion. In *Sākēt*, the idea of duty (*kartavya*) is not mechanical obedience but luminous participation in the cosmic order: each soul is a trustee of harmony.

Gupt's diction, steeped in the purity of Hindi-Sanskrit idiom, radiates this triad—*dharma, karuṇā, sevā*. He transforms the court of Ayodhya into a moral parliament of humankind. The citizen becomes worshipper; the ruler becomes servant. The city's splendour is not in gold or ritual, but in the even temper of conscience that knows no hierarchy before Truth.

II. *Sākēt* as a Human Gospel — From Myth to Morality

The greatness of *Sākēt* lies not in its adherence to myth but in its transmutation of it. Gupt's Rama and Sita are at once divine and deeply human. The epic moves from legend toward moral revelation—what may be called *a gospel of humanity*.

In Gupt's re-telling, exile becomes education, and suffering becomes sacrament. The forest is not a place of punishment but of purification; it is where civilization rediscovers the laws of compassion lost in the glitter of kingship. Sita's ordeal is no longer the spectacle of patriarchal trial—it is the crucible in which the feminine soul asserts moral equality with the masculine. Thus, *Sākēt* is India's first modern epic in which spirituality speaks the language of empathy rather than command.

The poet writes not to deify but to awaken. Every human heart, he suggests, carries within it the potential Ayodhya—a kingdom of self-rule founded on love. Through verse both simple and solemn, Gupt preaches an inward nationalism: freedom through virtue, and virtue through understanding. In this sense, *Sākēt* stands beside the scriptures of ethical renaissance—the *Bhagavad Gita* and the

Dhammapada—as a bridge between revelation and reform.

III. Comparison — Gupt ↔ Milton, Tagore, Tennyson

To the modern reader, Gupt may appear as the Milton of Hindi—majestic in moral gravity, austere in tone, and intent on reconciling liberty with obedience to divine order. Like Milton's *Paradise Lost*, *Sākēt* is not only an epic of God and man, but of the conscience of a nation. Both poets convert theology into moral psychology; both transform rebellion and exile into paths of illumination.

Yet Gupt's verse also carries the spiritual lyricism of Tagore. From Tagore he inherits the tenderness that perceives God as *Premaswaroopa*—Love embodied. The serenity of the Ganga echoes through his cadences, where devotion softens doctrine. If Milton gives us the justice of Heaven, Gupt gives us its compassion.

From Tennyson he learns the music of reflective sorrow—the disciplined metre that sustains melancholy without despair. Like Tennyson's *Idylls of the King*, *Sākēt* is an allegory of leadership, purity, and the fallibility of ideal men. But where

Tennyson's Camelot dissolves in doubt, Gupt's Ayodhya endures through faith: an unbroken horizon of moral sunrise.

Thus, Gupt stands at a luminous confluence: Milton's moral thunder, Tagore's mystic tenderness, Tennyson's measured elegance. Out of these elements he forges a uniquely Indian synthesis—an epic in which the Word becomes both revelation and revolution, a mirror of the eternal *Sākēt* that resides in the human heart.

NOTE ON THE TRANSCREATION

Sources Used — The Hindi Critical Editions

This English rendering of *Sākēt* is based primarily on the standard Lokbharti (Allahabad) and Sahitya Akademi editions of Maithili Sharan Gupt's text, collated with the Gita Press (Gorakhpur) reprints and the verified digital facsimile from the *Digital Library of India* (No. 2015.241745). In preparing this transcreation, occasional reference was made to the annotated editions of *Gupt Rachanavali* and commentaries published under the supervision of the Hindi Sahitya Sammelan (Prayag), to ensure textual accuracy and context for variant readings.

Since *Sākēt* evolved through successive printings between 1931 and 1958, minor orthographic differences (e.g., *अथं* vs *अथम्*, *ऊर्मिला* vs *ऊमिला*) have been normalized for consistency, without altering poetic sense. Wherever the text admitted ambiguity, preference has been given to readings that preserve rhythmic and emotional integrity rather than literal parallelism.

Verse Form, Diction, and Prosody

This English work is **not a prose translation**, but a **poetic transcreation** in elevated blank verse, inspired by the devotional–epic idiom of Milton and Tagore. Each canto reimagines Gupt's rhythm and bhāva through a flexible iambic or mixed cadence—allowing the verse to move freely between meditative narrative and lyrical invocation.

Where the original employs *chhandas* such as *doha*, *chaupaī*, *indravajra*, *upendravajra*, or *shārdūlavikrīḍita*, this English transcreation evokes the corresponding rhythm through natural stress patterns and inner cadence, rather than by mechanical metrical replication. The aim is *functional and emotional equivalence*—to preserve the dignity, tonal gravity, and spiritual resonance of Gupt's music within an idiom organic to English poetic speech.

The diction intentionally alternates between the **solemn** (for dharmic or philosophical passages) and the **lyrical** (for domestic or emotional scenes). Compound Sanskrit epithets are rendered into English compounds ("lotus-hearted queen," "truth-armoured prince") to retain both cadence and cultural colour. Archaisms are used sparingly, only where they echo Gupt's original gravitas.

Treatment of Indian Names and Philosophical Terms

All proper names from the Sanskrit–Hindi original are retained in their standard transliteration (*Rāma, Sītā, Lakṣmaṇa, Ayodhyā, Sāketa*), using macrons for long vowels where relevant in scholarly references, though in running text diacritics are often omitted (*Rama, Sita, Saket*) for readability.

Philosophical terms central to Gupt's vision—*Dharma, Karma, Bhakti, Tyāga, Karuṇā, Satya*—are kept untranslated, each explained briefly at first appearance and more fully in the **Glossary of Cultural and Philosophical Terms (Appendix II)**. This preserves the semantic density and spiritual precision that no single English word can convey.

Where metaphor demands interpretation rather than replication (for instance, *Agni-pariksha, Ram-rajya, Rāmrasa*), the English equivalent conveys the moral or emotional charge of the term, often with an explanatory note or in-text resonance.

In all cases, the goal has been not *conversion* but *communion*: to let the reader hear Gupt's music through an English lyre tuned to the same moral scale.

PART I – INVOCATION & PRELUDE

"O Muse of Light, awaken the heart to its vow; for every dawn is but remembrance of the first flame."

(Proem · Ayodhya as Moral Dawn)

INVOCATION

(Proem to SĀKET – The Devotional Epic)

O Muse of Dawn, who walk'st the sacred verge
Where mortal sorrow meets immortal calm,
Descend once more upon this speechless heart—
Not with the trumpet's blaze, but with a prayer.
Awake the veena of the soul, O Light,
That sang through Gupt, the seer of Sākēt's dream;
Let every string remember love through loss,
And echo Duty's music in the storm.

No sword I sing, nor empire's loud acclaim,
But the still conquest of the righteous mind;
How Love, by grief ennobled, learns to serve,
And Duty, touched by pity, turns divine.
Here is no war of kings, but hearts at war—
The crown of thorns more precious than of gold.
O Truth, whose throne is silence, lend me fire
To speak of man as mirror of the gods.

Hail, Rama—sun of gentleness and law,
Whose human tears redeem divinity;
Hail, Sita—flame of earth-born purity,
Who bore the world's injustice into grace.
Let every forest whisper of your calm,

Let every exile prove the soul's return.
May Ayodhya rise within each mortal breast,
Not built of marble, but of steadfast will.

If these frail words shall find one kindred ear,
And turn lament to reverent resolve,
Then not in vain this English lyre shall sound—
For love shall be its metre, faith its rhyme.
O Muse of Compassion, guide my trembling hand:
Let Sākēt live again—in human speech, divine.

PRELUDE: AYODHYA AS THE MORAL DAWN

Ayodhya was not merely a kingdom upon earth; it was the dawn of human conscience. In her streets, law did not command—it harmonized. Duty was not a burden; it was the fragrance of love made visible in action. The hum of the city at sunrise was the music of order freely embraced, where each citizen moved in rhythm with the unseen pulse of Dharma.

In that radiant age, the divine was not a distant sovereign but a presence woven through daily life. Every craft was a prayer; every gesture, a remembrance. To speak truth was to breathe the same air as the gods. The palace was but the echo of the hearth; the temple, but the mirror of the home. And upon this sacred plain, Rama was born—not to rule the world, but to awaken its heart.

Here begins the epic of *Sākēt*—not with conquest, but with concord; not with battle, but with balance. The poem opens in a world still unfallen, a world where beauty and duty walk hand in hand. Yet even as the light gathers, the shadow of exile stirs beyond the walls. For every moral dawn, like every sunrise, must prove its truth against the coming dark.

PART II – THE EIGHT CANTOS

"From harmony was born the law of love; and through each exile, the soul returns to light."

(The Epic Journey of Dharma and Compassion)

CANTO I – THE HOUSE OF AYODHYA

"O Mother of Light, awaken me to thy calm;
Let every dawn remember its own vow."

CANTO I – THE HOUSE OF AYODHYA

Theme: *Harmony, Beauty, and Love in the Age of Dharma*
Spirit: *A radiant world where art and virtue are one.*

Invocation

(In blank verse)

O Mother of Light, O Voice of the Sacred River,
awaken in me the measure of thy calm.
Teach my tongue to utter what heart remembers,
not as the pride of poets but the vow of sons.
For in thy city—bright Ayodhya—Truth
walked clothed in mortal grace; and every roof
was tuned to temple hymns, each hearth a shrine.
Give me, O Muse of Dharma, steady flame
to sing not splendour only but the soul—
the gentle pulse beneath the crown of kings,
the woman's faith, the brother's sleepless guard,
the quiet radiance where duty becomes love.

Let no false thunder of ambition sound;
let Beauty rise from service as from soil,
and Love be law, and law the heart of Love.
Bless this beginning, thou who dwell'st unseen
within the breath of every sacred name—
Sita, Urmila, Rama, Lakshmana—
whose lives were hymns to silence.
Grant me their peace; that I may tell
how Heaven once stooped to dwell in human ways,
and earth became the mirror of the Divine.

CANTO I – THE HOUSE OF AYODHYA

Prose Note (Context)

Ayodhya, the City of Dharma, awakens. Morning spreads like sanctity over golden towers; the people move in harmony with the rhythm of virtue. Within the palace, Urmila and Lakshmana speak in tender faith—their love not passion but worship. The moral sun of Ayodhya rises, heralding the age of harmony before exile and sorrow descend.

CANTO I – THE HOUSE OF AYODHYA

The Poem (Miltonic–Tagorian Free Verse)

Ayodhya rose like a song at dawn,
its towers breathing hymns of gold.
The river shone like wisdom made visible,
and every leaf repeated the syllables of peace.

From house to house, the fragrance of lamps
mingled with music and milk of prayer.
Mothers lifted their eyes to the morning star—
not to plead, but to thank.

Here, men were strong with gentleness;
women shone with strength made soft.
Children laughed as if to bless the dust,
and even the stones along the way
seemed taught to remember righteousness.

Within the palace hall, the air was still—
a stillness woven of lute and sandalwood.
Urmila, fair as the dawn of devotion,

bent her glance upon Lakshmana's face.
No words were fire, yet each was flame.
Between them glowed the hush of perfect trust,
as if two souls had found their single vow.

She said: "Beloved, all Ayodhya blooms today.
Duty walks crowned with joy.
But tell me, if the shadow falls,
shall thy vow still bloom in that dark soil?"

He answered with the quiet of a vow fulfilled:
"Where Rama walks, there is my path.
If His exile be the forest,
the forest shall be my heaven.
If His sorrow be the fire,
that fire shall be my lamp."

Urmila smiled, her tears the smile of strength.
"O Heart of Duty," she whispered, "go—
but leave with me thy song.
For even absence, when wedded to faith,
is presence made eternal."

Then through the corridors of the dawn
the conch of light was blown;
and Ayodhya stirred as if each brick
remembered its maker's prayer.

The city's breath became a single chant—
of beauty ripened into virtue,
of law made luminous by love.

And over it all, unseen but near,
the Voice of Dharma moved—
a wind through the golden flags,
singing to the sun:
**"This is the hour when men are gods,
and gods learn mercy through the hearts of men."**

Canto I – The House of Ayodhya

Poetic Commentary

In this opening canto, the world of Ayodhya shines as a vision of harmony where the moral and the aesthetic coalesce. Gupt's *Sākēt* begins not with a clash of powers, but with the stillness of ethical beauty. The devotion of Urmila and Lakshmana exemplifies the tenderness of dharma — duty embraced as love; love sanctified as discipline. In English transcreation, this canto restores the idea that civilization itself is an act of worship. Ayodhya here is not a place but a principle — a luminous order where every act becomes a prayer.

CANTO II – THE SHADOW OF EXILE

"Dharma walks barefoot, leaving gold behind;
The road becomes its altar."

CANTO II – THE SHADOW OF EXILE

Theme: *The Fall of Joy — from Palace to Wilderness*
Spirit: *How virtue is tested through love, and sorrow becomes the fire of truth.*

Invocation

(Blank verse, Miltonic–Tagorian tone)

O Lord of the Unswerving Heart,
whose will is calm amid the thunder of fate—
teach me to trace, in grief's darkened mirror,
the secret splendour of obedience.
For even the tear, when pure, is holy;
and even loss, when borne with faith, is gain.
Grant that I may see through sorrow's veil
the luminous face of Dharma walking unseen—
the patient step, the bowed yet steadfast brow
that turns from crown to dust without regret.
Let not pity weaken song, but sanctify it;
for the road to the forest is also the road to God.

CANTO II – THE SHADOW OF EXILE

Prose Note (Context)

The radiant world of Ayodhya trembles. Queen Kaikeyi's heart, once gentle, is stirred by pride and fear; her poisoned wish demands two boons — Rama's exile and Bharata's crown. King Dasharatha's soul breaks beneath the vow of his own lips. Rama accepts the decree with tranquil grace; Sita chooses exile over comfort; Urmila, in silent devotion, renounces joy for vigil. The city weeps as Dharma departs barefoot into the forest.

CANTO II – THE SHADOW OF EXILE

The Poem

(Miltonic–Tagorian free verse, rhythmic, luminous, devotional)

Night had fallen upon the House of Joy,
and within the jeweled chambers of Kaikeyi
envy awoke like a serpent in dream.
Soft words of a servant—dark as dew—
dropped poison into the honey of her heart.
Once her smile was a lamp in the king's hall,
now her brow grew clouded with imagined wrongs.

"Why," she whispered, "should Rama reign,
while my son waits in exile of affection?"
The goddess of reason fled her thought.
Desire sat on her throne.

When Dasharatha came, love-laden,
with eyes full of a father's joy,
she turned away, veiled in calculated grief.
He, trembling, asked— "What sorrow, my queen?"
She answered not in tears but in demand:
"Two boons you swore—redeem them now!"

The heavens held their breath.
"Speak, O beloved," said the king,
"ask what your heart would have—
for your wish is my vow."

"Then crown Bharata, and banish Rama
to the forest for fourteen years."

A silence like death stood between them.
Dasharatha's crown slid from his brow;
his voice broke as a shell upon the rock of fate.
"O merciless joy, thou art my ruin!" he cried.
But Kaikeyi's gaze was iron,
her heart, a frozen altar to ambition.

Then entered Rama—
serene as the moon upon stormy waters.
He heard, and smiled, as if hearing destiny's flute.
"Father," he said, "thy word is sacred law;
and mother's wish, the pathway of my feet.
The forest shall be my palace of peace,
and the leaves shall sing thy benediction."

Sita rose beside him, her eyes like prayer.
"Where thou goest, there goes my life," she said.
"The forest will bloom if I walk beside thee,
and exile shall be my bridal home."

Urmila, watching from the quiet threshold,
pressed her palms and spoke not.

But her silence glowed like a lamp unquenched—
for she who stays to guard love's absence
bears the heavier cross unseen.

At dawn, Ayodhya wept.
The streets were veiled in dust and tears.
Children clung to Rama's shadow,
elders laid their hearts upon the road.
Even the walls seemed to mourn,
their carvings dimmed by dew.

Dasharatha, bereft of his breath,
fell like a broken prayer at heaven's gate.
And Rama walked forth—calm, radiant, barefoot—
with Sita beside him, the embodiment of faith,
and Lakshmana, flame of devotion, guarding their path.

As the chariot crossed the city's edge,
a wind arose—not of storm, but of parting souls.
Ayodhya stood still, listening to the silence
that follows when virtue leaves the throne.

And somewhere, in the dust of that road,
a Voice, unseen yet eternal, whispered:
"Behold, Dharma walks out—
barefoot on the dust of the world."

CANTO II – THE SHADOW OF EXILE

Poetic Commentary

Here, the radiant order of Ayodhya yields to the austerity of exile — the moral night through which light learns its measure. Gupt's treatment of separation as purification is profound: suffering becomes the sacrament of realization. The transcreation retains this spiritual paradox — that the highest joy is born from obedience freely chosen. Exile is not punishment, but pilgrimage. The forest mirrors the heart, where every loss becomes an awakening, and every farewell, a form of faith.

CANTO III – THE FOREST AND THE INNER LIGHT

"Not wilderness, but wisdom blooms
where silence keeps its prayer."

CANTO III – THE FOREST AND THE INNER LIGHT

Theme: *Hermitage, Wisdom, and the Humanization of the Divine*
Spirit: *When God walks as man, the forest becomes scripture and silence turns to song.*

Invocation

(in Miltonic–Tagorian blank verse)

O Voice that speaks in leaves and flowing streams,
O Hidden Flame beneath the bark of time,
teach me the meaning of Thy quiet ways.
For now the City fades, and the soul must learn
the speech of wind, the patience of the soil.
Reveal, O Light within the wilderness,
how exile becomes a temple for the heart,
and solitude a greater brotherhood.

Let me behold Thee in the hermit's eye,
hear Thee in the rustle of unlearned prayer,
feel Thee in the tear that falls without desire.
Make my song not thunder, but deep air—

the living hush where Rama's calm abides,
and Sita's smile redeems the earth again.

CANTO III – THE FOREST AND THE INNER LIGHT

Prose Note (Context)

In the forest, Rama, Sita, and Lakshmana find sanctity in simplicity. The noise of Ayodhya yields to the music of leaves and rivers. Rama meets sages and seekers, learning from their austerity the deeper law—that Dharma is not a throne, but a way of being. Sita's compassion turns the forest to heaven; Lakshmana builds a hermitage where duty and love dwell side by side. Through silence and service, the divine becomes human, and the human divine.

CANTO III – THE FOREST AND THE INNER LIGHT

The Poem (Miltonic–Tagorian Epic Rendering)

Through shadowed paths and sunlit clearings they came,
three pilgrims clothed in the grace of renunciation.
No trumpet hailed them, no marble throne awaited—
only the whisper of the wind through tamal trees,
and the forest, vast as God's unspoken thought.

The birds sang hymns unscored by human hand;
each leaf bent low, as if to bless their steps.
Even the stones, old and moss-wrapped,
gleamed faintly as they passed,
like disciples remembering an ancient vow.

Rama, serene as morning on a mountain,
walked between his love and his brother—
the golden thread of harmony between devotion and strength.

No sorrow lay upon his brow,
only that radiant gravity which peace bestows
when it has been purchased through loss.

At Panchavati, they built their dwelling—
walls of woven grass, roof of patient toil.
Lakshmana's hands shaped the door of humility;
Sita spread the mat of worship with her smile.
There began the kingdom of the inward eye—
the republic of the soul.

The days moved slow as meditation;
the nights were vast with listening stars.
Rama spoke with hermits, their eyes bright
with that inward dawn that never sets.
"Lord," they said, "the forest is our scripture,
and silence is its verse.
In renunciation we find possession,
for the world is God's body, and we His breath."

Rama bowed—
for Wisdom humbles even the wise.
He saw in the austerity of the rishis
a mirror of his own heart:
the same still fire, the same unworded faith.

Sita walked beside the river,
her anklets soft as the murmur of prayer.
Wherever she gazed, the wilds grew gentle;
the thorns forgot to wound,
the beasts forgot their fear.
She gathered flowers not for adornment,

but for offering to the unseen.
Her hands, unstained by want,
became the emblem of compassionate power.

Lakshmana kept his vigil near,
a sentry of love that sleeps not.
His bow was silent, yet his eyes spoke fire:
"My brother's rest is my commandment;
my sister's smile, my faith."

Thus passed their exile—not in grief, but grace.
The forest became Ayodhya reborn—
without walls, without pride, yet rich with soul.

The sages came, bringing words of peace;
the deer approached, fearless as children;
the wind carried fragrance of unseen blossoms.
And the Lord of Life,
who had once ruled with sceptre and sword,
now ruled with stillness and a smile.

Then from afar a cry of the world arose—
of pain unhealed, of demons unchained.
The forest trembled;
its hymns turned into the prelude of battle.
Yet even in that foreboding hush,
the light of Rama's heart did not dim.

He said: "This forest is my teacher;
its silence, my scripture.

What I have learned here, I shall bear to the world—
that love is stronger than the wrath of gods."

And thus the wilderness, sanctified by their breath,
stood luminous beneath the timeless sky,
while unseen angels wrote upon the wind:
**"When Dharma walks the earth in humility,
even exile becomes enlightenment."**

CANTO III – THE FOREST AND THE INNER LIGHT

Poetic Commentary

In the still forest, the poem finds its meditative core. This canto transforms the wilderness into a temple of introspection. Rama's exile becomes a revelation — dharma stripped of splendour and clothed in silence. The English rendering deepens this idea through Miltonic cadence and inward music. Here, compassion matures into wisdom; renunciation is not denial, but illumination. Gupt's moral humanism thus anticipates modern ecological and ethical sensibilities alike — the forest as soul-space.

(These reflections are part of the transcreator's interpretive apparatus, intended to aid readers in perceiving the moral and spiritual structure of Gupt's Sākēt.)

CANTO IV – THE ABDUCTION OF SITA AND THE CRY OF THE SKY

"Faith, like a wounded bird, still flies
through sorrow's burning air."

CANTO IV – THE ABDUCTION OF SITA AND THE CRY OF THE SKY

Theme: *The Trial of Purity and the Feminine Voice*
Spirit: *Through the wound of loss, love reveals its eternal strength; through the silence of the wronged woman, the universe learns compassion.*

Invocation

(Miltonic–Tagorian blank verse)

O Breath of the Infinite, who dwellest unseen
in the faith of the steadfast and the grief of the pure,
teach me to speak of that stainless flame
which sorrow could not darken nor death divide.
Grant that my song may not weep for loss alone,
but praise the splendour of endurance—
the courage of the heart that breaks, yet blesses still.
Through Sita's trial let the world perceive
how love, when stripped of comfort, stands divine,

and womanhood becomes the conscience of creation.

CANTO IV – THE ABDUCTION OF SITA AND THE CRY OF THE SKY

Prose Note (Context)

The still peace of Panchavati ends. Ravana, the lord of darkness and pride, is drawn by lust and vengeance to the forest. Disguised as a mendicant, he deceives Sita and bears her away. Jatayu, the aged bird-sage, fights for her and falls. Rama and Lakshmana return to find the cottage empty— the earth widowed; the sky bereft of song. Sita's cry becomes the cry of the cosmos, and the trial of purity begins—not of guilt, but of endurance.

CANTO IV – THE ABDUCTION OF SITA AND THE CRY OF THE SKY

The Poem

(Miltonic–Tagorian free verse)

The forest slept beneath a noon of flame;
time seemed to breathe in golden pause.
The deer stood still as prayer incarnate,
the river hummed a mantra to itself.
Rama had gone in chase of phantom duty,
Lakshmana followed the echo of his call,
and silence held the hermitage like fate.

Then through the stillness came a shadowed sound—
the voice of a hermit, frail and begging bread.
Sita, ever tender, rose in pity's grace;
no fear could find a dwelling in her soul.
She crossed the threshold of protection's line,

the line of light her love had drawn—
not knowing that compassion can invite the storm.

Before her stood the mask of sanctity,
and behind it burned the eyes of greed.
Ravana, king of arrogance and pain,
bowed low in courtesy that mocked the gods.
"Lady," he said, "thy beauty shames the sun;
come, reign with me in Lanka's Isle of pearls."
She answered, calm as moonlight on a sword:
"My lord is Rama; my kingdom, his name.
Go, stranger, lest thy courtesy be curse."

Then pride became a tempest in his breast;
the earth shook with his wrath.
He seized her—like lightning binding flame—
and the air grew black with violated prayer.
The forest cried aloud; the heavens veiled their face.
From branch to branch the terror flew like wind,
till Jatayu, the agèd eagle, heard.

He rose, that ancient guardian of the right,
wings wide as vows fulfilled.
"O shame of kings!" he thundered through the air,
"Leave her, O Ravana, ere the sun itself turn dark!"
Steel met feather, power met age,
but spirit is stronger than sinew.
He fought till the heavens bled with feathers,
till his song became a psalm of dying faith.
Fallen, he whispered through a mist of blood:

“Tell Rama... she is gone toward the south...”—
and the sky received his soul like incense.

Evening returned with silence upon its brow.
Rama came, his heart still full of the forest’s peace,
and saw the door unguarded, the earth unlit.
He called—no echo answered.
He sought among the trembling leaves,
and every leaf replied with tears.
Then from afar he saw the scattered garland,
the broken pitcher, the fading footprints—
and knew that joy had left the world.

He cried her name, and the name became creation’s cry.
“Si-ta!”—the syllables rolled through heaven’s vaults,
and every living thing grew still to hear.
The wind wept through the trees,
the river forgot its song;
even the sun dimmed his aureate crown.

Lakshmana stood beside him, struck to stone.
No warrior’s pride remained, no brother’s speech—
only that dreadful, shining silence
which is the body of the soul’s despair.

Then Rama knelt upon the ground of loss
and placed his palm upon the earth.
“O Mother,” he said, “guard Thou her form.

O Dharma, keep her faith inviolate.
For though my eyes may fail to see her now,
her truth shall be the lamp of all the worlds."

And from the horizon came a low response—
not wind, not thunder, but the grief of heaven itself:
"The pure are never lost; they live as light,
and light returns through sorrow to the One."

Thus fell the day that ended joy,
and thus began the night of revelation.
For in her bondage Sita held the seed of freedom;
and in his anguish Rama learned the weight of love.
Between them stretched the world's long exile—
the distance every soul must cross to find itself again.

And over that darkening forest
moved an unseen radiance, solemn, slow,
as though the very stars were writing in their fire:
"Through the tears of the blameless
shall the gods remember mercy."

CANTO IV – THE ABDUCTION OF SITA AND THE CRY OF THE SKY

Poetic Commentary

This is the canto of ordeal, where Sītā's suffering becomes the moral axis of the epic. Gupt reclaims her from passive sorrow into active sanctity — the conscience of *Sākēt* itself. The "cry of the sky" is both personal and cosmic: the voice of violated innocence demanding remembrance, not revenge. In English verse, this moment expands into a universal archetype — the eternal feminine standing firm against chaos. Dharma is tested, but not defeated; its silence speaks louder than conquest.

(These reflections are part of the transcreator's interpretive apparatus, intended to aid readers in perceiving the moral and spiritual structure of Gupt's Sākēt.)

CANTO V – THE DEVOTION OF SHABARI AND THE MEETING WITH HANUMAN

“Each tear a seed of worship sown
in soil made holy by waiting.”

CANTO V – THE DEVOTION OF SHABARI AND THE MEETING WITH HANUMAN

Theme: *Faith, Service, and the Rediscovery of Hope*

Spirit: *The forest, once dark with loss, is illumined again by love's humility. In the heart of the lowly devotee and the fearless servant, Rama rediscovers the rhythm of divine purpose.*

Invocation

(Miltonic–Tagorian blank verse)

O Thou who hidest splendour in the dust,
whose kingdom blossoms in the hands of the poor,
teach me to praise not power but purity.
Let this song breathe of huts more holy than thrones,
of broken hearts that keep unbroken faith.

For in the sweetness of Shabari's fruit,
in the service of the wind-born son,
Thy truth descends again among the weary.
Grant me the voice to tell how Love, forgotten,
finds itself anew in devotion's smile—
and how hope, like dawn, is born from ashes.

CANTO V – THE DEVOTION OF SHABARI AND THE MEETING WITH HANUMAN

Prose Note (Context)

After Sita's abduction, Rama and Lakshmana wander through the southern forests seeking her. In the hermitage of Shabari—an aged devotee awaiting his coming—Rama finds solace and blessing. Her offering of wild fruits becomes a sacrament of love beyond caste and ritual. Later, on the banks of Pampa, Rama meets Hanuman, messenger of Sugriva and emblem of perfect service. Through these encounters, despair turns to faith, and exile becomes mission.

CANTO V – THE DEVOTION OF SHABARI AND THE MEETING WITH HANUMAN

The Poem

(Miltonic–Tagorian free verse; meditative, luminous, devotional)

Through forests veined with sunset gold they came,
two pilgrims bearing silence as their crown.
The path was strewn with thorns of memory;
each step a wound, yet each wound a prayer.

Upon a slope of tamarind and flame-tree stood
a hut of woven grass, humble as hope itself.
There Shabari dwelt—
her hair a silver river of long waiting,
her eyes bright with the patience of the dawn.

Each dawn she swept the threshold of her faith,
each eve she set her little earthen lamp
for the unseen feet of her Beloved.

"Will He not come today?" she whispered to the trees.
The trees replied with rustling benediction,
and still she waited—years turned to lifetimes.

Then one morning the air grew tremulous,
as if the forest breathed a vow fulfilled.
Rama came—dust upon his brow,
sorrow upon his smile—and the world grew still.
Shabari fell before him, weeping joy;
not as one who worships a god afar,
but as a child who finds her mother's hand.

"Rise, blessed one," said Rama gently,
"thy love has outworn time itself.
I have come, not to grant, but to learn—
for thy waiting is a scripture I must read."

She offered him fruit, each one tested on her lips,
sweetness proven by devotion's taste.
The sages watched from heaven's edge and smiled;
for purity, they knew, is its own commandment.

He ate, and the forest bloomed again;
even the withered leaves turned tender green.
Lakshmana bowed, his stern eyes moist:
"O brother, she is the mirror of thy faith."

Then Rama said to Shabari,
"Thy hut is holier than Indra's hall;

for where love dwells without pride,
there dwells the Lord unseen."

She bowed, her soul already winged.
"Go forth," she said, "to the lake of Pampa;
there waits the friend of monkeys, the child of the wind.
Through him thy hope shall learn to soar."
Her body sank, but her voice remained,
floating in the air like incense after flame.

Southward they went,
and the forest widened into water and sky.
By the calm of Pampa's crystal breast
Rama sat and gazed—his reflection
half sorrow, half awakening light.
Then came Hanuman, swift yet humble,
his eyes lit with the clarity of service.

He bowed— "My Lord, I am the servant of the truth
you carry in your silence.
Sugriva, my king, seeks refuge in your grace."

Rama looked and saw not ape nor man,
but the soul of duty made visible.
"Arise," he said, "faith has taken form in thee.
Lead me where purpose waits reborn."

Hanuman rose, a smile of flame on his lips.
Around them stirred the breath of destiny.
The air itself grew resolute with promise;
even sorrow seemed to lift its head.

Thus hope returned, not as thunder, but as dawn.
Through the tears of the poor and the strength of the pure,
the road to Lanka began.
No longer exile, but pilgrimage;
no longer grief, but consecrated will.

And the voice of heaven whispered through the wind:
"When the humble serve, the lost are found, and the Infinite bends close to hear their song."

CANTO V – THE DEVOTION OF SHABARI AND THE MEETING WITH HANUMAN

Poetic Commentary

This canto marks a turn from grief to grace. *Shabarī's* humble devotion and *Hanumān's* service embody bhakti as action, not sentiment. Gupt's genius lies in making spiritual love tangible — a movement of will, a rhythm of loyalty. The English transcreation mirrors this devotional energy through meditative imagery and restrained exaltation. Here, faith walks; it does not wait. Every act becomes offering, and every breath, remembrance. The forest turns from exile into ashram — a garden of awakened hearts.

(These reflections are part of the transcreator's interpretive apparatus, intended to aid readers in perceiving the moral and spiritual structure of Gupt's Sākēt.)

CANTO VI – THE ALLIANCE WITH SUGRĪVA, SĪTĀ'S MESSAGE, AND THE BRIDGE OF FAITH

"Hope builds its bridge of prayer
across the sea of doubt."

CANTO VI – THE ALLIANCE WITH SUGRĪVA, SĪTĀ'S MESSAGE, AND THE BRIDGE OF FAITH

Theme: *Fellowship, Divine Strategy, and the Building of Hope Across the Sea*
Spirit: *Out of sorrow rises purpose, and through fellowship the human becomes divine. The bridge to Lanka is not of stones alone, but of hearts bound in trust.*

Invocation

(In Miltonic–Tagorian blank verse)

O Lord of the Lonely Path,
whose exile is Thy glory,
breathe strength into the weary dust of man.
Let every friendship be a sacrament of trust,
and every labour an altar of faith.
From the cry of the wind and the roar of the sea
fashion anew the bridge between heaven and earth,
where duty and love clasp hands over the abyss.
Grant that I may sing of comradeship divine—
of the meeting of souls that build what storms
cannot destroy.

CANTO VI – THE ALLIANCE WITH SUGRĪVA, SĪTĀ'S MESSAGE, AND THE BRIDGE OF FAITH

Prose Note (Context)

After meeting Hanuman, Rāma is brought to Sugrīva, the exiled king of the Vānaras. Their alliance is born of mutual sorrow and mutual faith: one seeks a wife, the other a throne. With Hanuman's leap to Lanka and the discovery of Sītā, hope turns to destiny. Then begins the mighty labour—the building of the Setu, the bridge of stones and vows—a symbol of unity between the divine and the human will.

CANTO VI – THE ALLIANCE WITH SUGRĪVA, SĪTĀ'S MESSAGE, AND THE BRIDGE OF FAITH

The Poem

(Miltonic–Tagorian free verse)

In the glades of Rishyamūkha met the two,
each king in sorrow, yet rich in worth.
Their eyes held the memory of broken realms,
their hearts the hunger of righteousness.
Rāma spoke, his voice a calm that ruled grief:
"Brother, thy pain is mine; our wounds are one.
Thou seekest thy crown, I my beloved—
both lost to treachery, both vowed to truth.
Let us unite, and heaven shall bend toward us."

Sugrīva bowed; his brow touched dust and tears.
"The forest shall be thy fortress and my throne.
Together we shall lift our wrongs to right."

And the wind-borne Hanuman stood between
them—
a flame of faith, kindled by love's breath.
Around them stirred the leaf and stream,
as if the forest knew a covenant divine.

Then came the trial of friendship:
Rāma's arrow struck the mighty Vāli down,
and the silence after rang with fate.
The hills echoed with the cry of justice,
not wrath, but law fulfilled in light.
For Rāma's bow was mercy shaped as strength,
and the slain rose free from sin's long sleep.

Sugrīva wept, yet wisdom rose through grief.
"The just are terrible, yet kind," he said.
And taking up the golden crown of trust,
he ruled not self, but service to his friend.

The rains came down, perfumed and pure,
and Rāma waited by the southern shore.
Each drop that fell was a reminder of tears,
each thunder-roll, a summons to resolve.
Then Hanuman leapt—
not merely across the sea,
but across the gulf of despair.
The winds bowed before him,
the clouds held him in their arms.

In the palace of Lanka's dread,
he found the lotus captive, Sītā pale and calm—
a prayer imprisoned, yet unbroken flame.
Her eyes held faith like moonlight caught in bars.
"Tell him," she said, "my love is not a cry,
but a commandment carved in silence.
Let him come not in rage, but in truth."

He touched her feet—
and all the demons in the dark drew back.
Then, like a torch returning to the dawn,
he flew with tidings of the heart's sunrise.

By the ocean now stood Rāma still,
the waves repeating her name in whispers.
Within him the gods of patience stirred;
within the sea, the gods of resistance slept.
He prayed—his voice was thunder made tender:
"O Lord of depths, thou mirror of my vow,
yield way to love, or bear the weight of justice."

The waters rose, then bowed—
for even oceans serve the just.
Then came Nala, the builder sage,
and the hosts of vanaras, strong as faith.
They carried mountains as men carry dreams,
casting them upon the sea with laughter.
Each stone sank, then floated—
for when hearts are pure, even matter obeys.

Day by day, the Setu grew—
a hymn in rock, a psalm in labour.

And as they built, each name of Rāma
was written upon the waves by wind.

Upon that bridge of hope and toil
the dawn of destiny began to rise.
No longer were the exiles homeless—
for where love works, there is homeland.
Sītā's voice called from across the sea;
Rāma's faith answered through the stones.

The sky bent low, garlanded with clouds,
and the world knew that a new covenant had begun—
not of gods ruling men,
but of men becoming divine through service.

And from the foam of the ocean came a whisper:
"Faith builds what the proud can never cross—for the sea yields only to love."

CANTO VI – THE ALLIANCE WITH SUGRĪVA, SĪTĀ'S MESSAGE, AND THE BRIDGE OF FAITH

Poetic Commentary

This canto celebrates the fraternity of righteousness. The alliance between Rāma and Sugrīva, and the building of the bridge, symbolize dharma's constructive power — faith as architecture. The bridge is both literal and spiritual: an act of collaboration between mortals and the divine ideal within them. The English verse reflects this through imagery of cooperation and luminous resolve. Gupt's vision anticipates the Gandhian ethos of unity in moral purpose — strength born of service.

(These reflections are part of the transcreator's interpretive apparatus, intended to aid readers in perceiving the moral and spiritual structure of Gupt's Sākēt.)

CANTO VII – THE WAR OF LANKA AND THE FALL OF RĀVAṆA

"Justice, like thunder, breaks in light;
the sword becomes a flame of truth."

CANTO VII – THE WAR OF LANKA AND THE FALL OF RĀVAṆA

Theme: *The Fire of Dharma, the Trial of Power, and the Redemption through Justice*
Spirit: *Where righteousness confronts pride, and divine strength is tempered by compassion. The war becomes a revelation — not of destruction, but of deliverance.*

Invocation

(in Miltonic–Tagorian blank verse)

O Eternal Flame, who burnest not to consume but to cleanse,
breathe upon my song the light of thy justice.
Let wrath be transfigured into compassion,
and the sword become a beam of truth.
Grant me to sing not of conquest, but of the cleansing fire
that restores the balance of worlds.
Where the proud fall, let mercy arise;
where blood is spilt, let stars be born.

CANTO VII – THE WAR OF LANKA AND THE FALL OF RĀVAṆA

Prose Note (Context)

The hosts of Rāma cross the ocean by the bridge of faith and reach the golden isle of Lanka. There, arrogance and adoration confront one another. Rāvaṇa's splendour—his genius, his music, his power—is darkened by pride. The great battle begins: a cosmic struggle between dharma and desire. In its thunder, all human destinies echo the same law—that strength must kneel before truth, and even evil may find redemption through surrender.

CANTO VII – THE WAR OF LANKA AND THE FALL OF RĀVAṆA

The Poem

(Miltonic–Tagorian free verse)

When dawn rose crimson on the sea's far rim,
the earth trembled as the hosts awoke.
The vanaras beat their drums upon the sand,
and mountains answered with a thousand cries.
Before them stood the towers of Lanka—
burnished gold, proud in the sun's disdain.
Rāma beheld them, and his gaze was still,
as one who sees beyond the day's bright pride.
He turned to the sea and said in silence:
"O Lord, who setteth boundaries to waves,
let justice too have measure in its wrath."

Hanuman leapt to the gates like thunder,
and Angada spoke with a voice of flame:
"Yield, Rāvaṇa! Restore the stolen light!
Bow to the one whose mercy mirrors heaven!"
But pride is deaf when heart is dark.

Rāvaṇa's laughter rolled across the spires—
a tempest forged of music and despair.

Within the palace, Mandodari wept:
"Thy glory is enough, my lord—why war with truth?"
But he, whose ten crowns held the weight of worlds,
heard not the tremor of her faithful tears.
"Shall I, who raised the heavens on my will,
bend before a forest prince?" he said.
And thus the titan sealed his fate.

Then battle rose—a dance of fire and thunder.
The sky turned bronze; the earth grew white with dust.
Each shout was a mountain falling,
each arrow, a streak of time itself.
Lakṣmaṇa fought like the lightning of justice,
cleaving through illusion's mist.
Hanuman bore the wounded to safety
as wind carries prayer to the unseen.
And Rāma—serene amidst the storm—
stood like the axis of the turning world.

The gods leaned down upon the wind;
their tears became rain upon the field.
Even the demons, struck by awe, paused—
for never had they seen such beauty in wrath.

Each shaft that left his bow sang like a psalm;
each stroke was mercy dressed as flame.

Then rose the night of dread encounter.
Rāvaṇa, vast as fate, came forth.
Ten faces crowned the gloom like suns defiled,
each burning with knowledge turned to pride.
The air was black with power;
his roar broke mountains into prayer.
Before him stood the calm of dharma—
the bow drawn, the eyes like pity's flame.

"Return," said Rāma softly,
"for even now grace waits upon thy soul.
Thou art mighty, but might is not thine own;
it is the loan of heaven, repaid in love."
But pride is blind to mercy's voice.
The tenfold shadow answered with a storm.

Then light and darkness clashed.
The heavens shook with the cry of elements.
Each thunderbolt that fell from Rāma's bow
was a syllable of cosmic law.
Through every roar and burst of fire
the universe learned the cost of freedom.

At last the arrow—the Brahmāstra bright—
sped singing through the storm of years.
It struck, and silence bloomed like dawn.
The crowns fell one by one,
and with them pride and sorrow broke.

The earth breathed again, as if long held breath
returned to the heart of creation.

Rāvaṇa fell—not damned, but delivered.
His eyes, now clear of passion's dust,
beheld in death the face of grace.
"Lord," he whispered, "I fought Thee long,
but in Thee I find my rest."
Rāma bowed, and the world wept not for triumph,
but for the beauty of repentance.

Upon the field the winds grew still.
The vanaras knelt, their hearts in flame and awe.
And from the ashen sky came voices of the gods:
"Thus ends not war, but begins peace—
for dharma is not vengeance but restoration."

Then Rāma turned to the sea and said,
"The bridge endures, but not of stone—
it is the bridge of hearts that span the void."
He lifted his gaze toward Lanka's throne,
and in that moment power itself bowed down.

Thus fell the proud, thus rose the just;
and heaven learned anew its law—
that conquest is but the shadow of compassion,
and every death a seed of life.

CANTO VII – THE WAR OF LANKA AND THE FALL OF RĀVAṆA

Poetic Commentary

In this canto, war is no longer a spectacle of violence, but a moral revelation. Gupt redefines heroism as self-mastery; the true battle is within. The English transcreation keeps this gravity, translating combat into conscience. Every strike of the bow is weighed against the scale of compassion. When victory comes, it is not triumphal but purgative — dharma reaffirmed through restraint. The battlefield thus becomes a mirror of the soul's inner trial, echoing both the *Gītā* and modern humanist ethics.

(These reflections are part of the transcreator's interpretive apparatus, intended to aid readers in perceiving the moral and spiritual structure of Gupt's Sākēt.)

CANTO VIII – THE RETURN TO AYODHYA AND THE DAWN OF RĀMA–RĀJYA

"Peace descends as duty's flower;
the crown returns to conscience."

CANTO VIII – THE RETURN TO AYODHYA AND THE DAWN OF RĀMA–RĀJYA

Theme: *Restoration, Peace, and the Reign of the Inner Dharma*
Spirit: *The journey from exile to home becomes the journey from suffering to wisdom. In this canto, joy is no longer the mirth of victory, but the stillness of realized love.*

Invocation

(in Miltonic–Tagorian blank verse)

O Spirit of the Returning Light,
Thou who makest the wound a doorway of grace,
let my song be a garland for the feet of peace.
For even after fire, the earth remembers bloom;
and after exile, the heart rediscovers home.
Teach us, O Eternal Presence,
that every loss fulfilled Thy plan,
and that dharma, when completed, becomes love.

CANTO VIII – THE RETURN TO AYODHYA AND THE DAWN OF RĀMA–RĀJYA

Prose Note (Context)

After the great war, Rāma, Sītā, and Lakṣmaṇa return from Lanka to Ayodhya, borne upon the chariot of time and faith. Bharata, who has ruled as servant and brother, awaits them with the sandals of the Lord upon the throne. The city, once shrouded in grief, awakens to the golden music of reunion. Yet the victory is inward: the triumph of dharma over despair, of compassion over pride. In this canto, Gupt's vision of *Sākēt* becomes universal — the dawn of divine order not in power, but in love.

CANTO VIII – THE RETURN TO AYODHYA AND THE DAWN OF RĀMA–RĀJYA

The Poem

(Miltonic–Tagorian free verse)

The long years folded like petals of a dream,
and the dust of sorrow turned to dawn.
Through clouds of incense and memory,
the chariot moved upon the wind of joy.
Hanuman, still humble in victory,
guided the steeds like prayers released.
And on the horizon rose Ayodhya—
no city of brick, but of remembrance.
Its towers glimmered like hymns reborn,
its streets a river of awaiting hearts.

Bharata stood before the gates,
his brow unshorn, his garments austere.
Upon the vacant throne he had placed the sandals—

symbols of the absent Lord.
For fourteen years they ruled in silence,
and the kingdom breathed through devotion alone.

When he saw the returning chariot gleam,
he fell—not in despair but awe.
"My duty ends," he said,
"but my service is eternal."
Rāma raised him, saying softly:
"Brother, thou hast fulfilled what even kings forget—
that rule is worship when self is gone."

The people poured like rivers toward the gates,
each heart a bell, each tear a spark.
The mothers sang of sons redeemed;
the old recalled their youth in faith.
Sītā came forth, radiant yet still—
as if the world itself had bowed within her gaze.
And from her hands fell flowers upon the earth,
which blossomed where they touched.

Ayodhya woke as heaven's mirror.
Every home was an altar, every lamp a star.
No cry of hunger, no wound of greed remained;
even beasts of field and forest lived in gentle accord.
Justice walked unclothed, needing no sword,
for law was love, and love was the only law.

Rāma reigned—not as monarch, but as meaning.
His glance became the measure of right,
his silence the scripture of peace.
He held not sceptre but balance,
where mercy outweighed wrath.
The humblest voice was heard as prayer;
the strongest heart was softened into song.
Temples rose not of marble but of memory,
and dharma was written upon the pulse of men.

Thus dawned the age they called *Rāma–Rājya*—
not a kingdom, but a way of being.
In every hut and heart there burned the same small flame
that lit the throne of the Eternal City.
And Sākēt —Ayodhya of the soul—
became the symbol of what man may be,
when heaven is not beyond but within.

At evening, when the lamps were lit,
Rāma and Sītā walked alone upon the terrace.
The sky leaned low, veiled in soft gold.
She said, "Beloved, the war is past—
but the greater task remains:
to keep the peace within."
He smiled, as only one who knows both exile and return may smile,
and placed her hand within his own.

The moon rose over Ayodhya's towers—
a silver vow upon the brow of earth.

The river shone like truth fulfilled,
and in that stillness heaven bowed to man.
The wind carried a whisper through the stars:

"Thus ends the exile of the world;
thus begins the reign of the soul."

Epilogue

So, ends *Sākēt*—not in battle, but in benediction. Rāma's journey is the heart's own pilgrimage, from ignorance to insight, from law to love. In him the divine became human, that the human might become divine. And in the city called *Ayodhya*—the unassailable dwelling of peace—the spirit of India found its mirror and its song.

CANTO VIII – THE RETURN TO AYODHYA AND THE DAWN OF RĀMA–RĀJYA

Poetic Commentary

The closing canto restores harmony — not through restoration of empire, but through the redemption of the human spirit. *Rāma's* return is less political than metaphysical: the homecoming of truth to its rightful throne within the heart. In English form, the verse attains elegiac calm, completing the journey from light to light. Gupt's Ayodhya thus transcends history and geography; it becomes the eternal Sākēt — the state of compassion realized through discipline, where love fulfils its dharma.

(These reflections are part of the transcreator's interpretive apparatus, intended to aid readers in perceiving the moral and spiritual structure of Gupt's Sākēt.)

PART III — THE CLOSING VISON

"And the song returned to silence,
but the silence remembered the song."

(Epilogue · Author's Colophon · Afterword)

EPILOGUE: THE ETERNAL SĀKET

(A reflective coda in Miltonic–Tagorian blank verse)

The Poem

Not ended is the tale, though peace has come;
no city stands forever in its stone.
For Sākēt was not wrought of rock or gold,
but of a vision that outlives its walls.
When Dharma walked in human guise,
the world beheld its own forgotten height;
and every heart became a lesser Ayodhya,
a shrine unbuilt, yet ever lit within.

The ages pass; the river changes name;
and kingdoms fade like evening chants in dust.
Yet still the unseen chariot moves through time,
bearing the Lord of the Quiet Flame—
He who governs not by fear but by forgiveness,
He who conquers not by sword but by soul.

Wherever justice kneels beside compassion,
wherever strength bends humbly to protect,
wherever a ruler listens before he commands—
there breathes the fragrance of Rāma's reign.
The bridge of faith is never wholly lost;
its stones are hearts that choose to serve.

And Sītā's voice, that tender vow of earth,
still whispers through the sighing of the fields—
that purity is not of body, but of being;
that woman's courage is the conscience of man.
Her silence echoes louder than the drums of war,
and teaches love its final art: to endure.

Urmilā's waiting is the world's long patience,
Lakṣmaṇa's vigil, the mind's unyielding guard;
Bharata's rule, the heart's obedience to the good;
and Hanumān's leap, the soul's unmeasured faith.
All these return in every age of need,
wearing new names, yet bearing the same light.

The poet stands upon the dust of years,
and sees no vanquished Lanka, no lost dawn—
only the pilgrim spirit moving on,
from fire to freedom, exile to return.
O men of later days, rebuild your Sākēt here,
not in marble domes nor iron laws,
but in the speech of truth, the deed of kindness,
the breath that forgives before it wounds.

For heaven is not a realm apart from pain,
but the ripened fruit of a heart made whole.
And when man learns again to walk in peace,
not proud of right but grateful for it—
then shall Ayodhya rise anew,
not in the East alone, but everywhere:

a city unbesieged, unaging, undestroyed—
the dwelling of the Eternal Man within the soul of God.

Closing Inscription

Thus ends the song of Sākēt—
not the end of an age, but its remembrance.
For each who lives by truth and love,
the gates of Ayodhya never close.

AFTERWORD

Reflections on Sākēt as an Epic of Compassion

(The Relevance of Rāma's Dharma in the Modern World)

There are works that record the deeds of kings, and there are others that redeem the hearts of men. *Sākēt* belongs to the latter. It is not merely an epic of exile and return; it is a scripture of compassion written in the idiom of poetry. Through its eight cantos, the radiant world of Ayodhya rises and falls, yet within that rhythm of joy and sorrow, one constant shines—the quiet majesty of Dharma, not as law, but as love made luminous.

Gupt's *Sākēt* is not content to glorify the heroic; it humanizes the divine. His Rāma is not the inaccessible god of temples but the awakened conscience of humanity. His Sītā is not merely the consort of virtue but its living flame—the embodiment of endurance, purity, and forgiveness. In their trials and silences, we glimpse the eternal conflict of the human soul between justice and mercy, between the outer rule and the inner call.

To modern readers, burdened by the noise of progress and the exile of meaning, *Sākēt* speaks like a voice remembered from childhood—soft, sorrowful, yet strong enough to rebuild faith. It teaches that Dharma is not a code but a consciousness; that righteousness without tenderness becomes tyranny; and that the truest victory is not over others, but over oneself.

In an age divided by politics, creed, and the fever of possession, the moral vision of *Sākēt* stands as a quiet counterpoint. It calls upon us to rebuild Ayodhya not in marble or myth, but in the mind. The *Ram-Rājya* of Gupt is not a nostalgic kingdom—it is the kingdom of equilibrium, where reason bows to reverence, and strength to compassion.

The modern world, so rich in invention and so poor in wisdom, needs the language of *Sākēt* more than ever. Its verses remind us that civilization is not sustained by power, but by pity; not by triumph, but by trust. The true heir of Rāma is not the ruler, but the listener—the one who hears in every cry of pain a call to serve, and in every stranger's face the reflection of the divine.

If this English transcreation, inspired by Gupt's immortal Hindi, can awaken even a single spark of that ancient tenderness in the heart of today's reader, it will have fulfilled its sacred purpose. For *Sākēt* is not a monument to the past, but a mirror held to the present—a reminder that the kingdom of compassion has never fallen; it only waits to be remembered.

> *"For Dharma is not a crown upon the*
> *brow of kings—*
> *it is the pulse of mercy beating in the*
> *breast of man."*

From the Transcreator's Journal

Composed at dawn, when the first rays touched the manuscript, and the air still carried the fragrance of devotion. May every reader who turns these pages find within them not merely the story of Rāma, but the remembrance of their own inner Ayodhya.

on the completion of the English transcreation of Sākēt

— **Anand Kumar Ashodhiya**
Transcreator of SĀKET
Avikavani Publishers, 2025

AUTHOR'S COLOPHON

(A Farewell to the Readers)

When the song grew silent, I found it still singing within— not mine, but the voice of the ages that speak through love. In shaping this English *Sākēt*, I have merely held a lamp to the vast horizon where Maithili Sharan Gupt once stood, seeing in the dusk of his nation the dawn of its soul.

This work is not a translation, but a pilgrimage in verse— a walk beside those timeless pilgrims of Ayodhya:

Rāma, who forgave before he judged;
Sītā, who endured before she spoke;
Lakṣmaṇa, who served before he slept;
and Bharata, who ruled only to renounce.

If I have re-told their journey in another tongue, it is that the English ear, too, may hear the Sanskrit of the heart—the soundless syllable of truth. For poetry is not the art of words, but the remembrance of light; and faith, when uttered in any language, is but the soul's translation of silence.

May this book serve not as a monument, but as a mirror— that each who reads may see, within his own life, a little of Sākēt: a realm of peace, where duty is devotion and compassion is law. If such vision awakens even for a moment, the labour of this poet is fulfilled.

I close, therefore, as Gupt himself might have closed— not with pride of completion, but with prayer for worthiness:

> *Let my words be fewer than my*
> *reverence, my thought humbler than*
> *my theme.*
> *For the Spirit of Sākēt is not to be*
> *written—it must be lived.*

— The Transcreator and Devotee of the Eternal Ayodhya

PART IV APPENDICES AND SCHOLARLY NOTES

(Supplementary and Reference Materials for Readers and Scholars)

"Where poetry becomes reflection, and devotion becomes understanding."

(Selected Verses · Glossarial Notes · Chronology · References)

APPENDIX I
CRITICAL EVALUATION / ACADEMIC REVIEW

SĀKET — An English Transcreation

By **Anand Kumar Ashodhiya**
(Avikavani Publishers, 2025)
Reviewed by **Dr Babu Ram (D.Litt.)**
Professor and Chairperson, Department of Hindi, Baba Mast Nath University, Rohtak, Haryana

The Epic Reborn: Between Translation and Revelation

In the landscape of modern Indian letters, *SĀKET — An English Transcreation* by Anand Kumar Ashodhiya represents a rare literary achievement: an attempt to lift the ethical and devotional spirit of Maithili Sharan Gupt's *Sākēt* into the dignified resonance of English blank verse. It is not a literal translation but an act of poetic rebirth—a **transcreation**, where English becomes the sacred vessel for Gupt's moral imagination. Ashodhiya stands at the confluence of two great traditions: Milton's moral grandeur and Tagore's spiritual lyricism. The result is a devotional epic that speaks across civilizations.

Poetic Architecture and Voice

Structured in **eight Cantos**, the work mirrors the moral arc of Gupt's *Sākēt*—from the harmony of Ayodhya to the redemption of exile. The language adopts **Miltonic blank verse**, solemn and meditative, yet infused with the lyrical tenderness of Tagore.

"Ayodhya rose like a song at dawn,
its towers breathing hymns of gold."

The measured rhythm, luminous diction, and Sanskritic imagery—*Dharma,* Sākēt*, Rāma, Sītā*—give the poem a contemplative aura. Ashodhiya's verse restores to English that sacred cadence once found in *Paradise Lost*, *The Prelude*, and *Gitanjali.*

Dharma as Poetic Consciousness

Where Western epics glorify conquest, *SĀKET* glorifies **conscience**. Rāma's greatness lies not in triumph but in **restraint**; Sītā's in **endurance made luminous**. The poem transforms *dharma* into poetic consciousness—

"Let Beauty rise from service as from soil,
and Love be law, and law the heart of Love."

Thus, dharma becomes not doctrine but discipline — a harmony of action and compassion, of ethics and aesthetics.

A Humanist Scripture

Ashodhiya's transcreation revives Gupt's essential humanism. Here, the divine is not remote but reflected in the ordinary: the brother's vigil, the wife's silence, the exile's calm. The English *SĀKET* becomes a *modern scripture of compassion*, where devotion is not a ritual act but a moral awakening.

"If His sorrow be the fire,
that fire shall be my lamp."

This verse captures the Indian ethos — serenity amid duty, humility amid strength.

Language, Style, and Structure

Each Canto opens with an invocation, followed by a brief prose context, and culminates in a sustained poetic rendering. This structure blends epic scope with lyrical intimacy, making the work accessible to international readers. The poet's use of Sanskritic resonances and Vedic symbolism—*the forest of prayer, the lamp of compassion, the chariot of renunciation*—grounds the work in the civilizational idiom of India while allowing universal comprehension.

Comparative Significance

In comparative poetics, Ashodhiya's *SĀKET* occupies a unique position:

- Like **Milton**, it celebrates the freedom of moral will.
- Like **Tagore**, it consecrates beauty as the medium of love.
- Like **Gupt**, it transforms myth into moral philosophy.

The synthesis of these lineages yields a new epic genre—**the humanist devotional poem**, where art and ethics coalesce.

Cultural and Academic Value

This transcreation serves multiple audiences:

• For **academics**, it demonstrates transcreation as a legitimate literary form, bridging translation and original composition.

• For **cultural historians**, it reanimates the moral universe of the Rāmāyaṇa in modern idiom.

• For **general readers**, it offers an English work of rare serenity and ethical beauty.

The inclusion of appendices—Hindi stanzas, glossary, chronology—further enhances its utility for comparative literature and Indology studies.

Conclusion: The Modern Ayodhya

In an era of fragmentation, *SĀKET — An English Transcreation* restores the forgotten harmony between beauty and virtue. It teaches that dharma is not law imposed, but **love disciplined**; that divinity is not escape, but **embodied awareness**. Through this work, Ayodhya becomes once again not a city, but a state of being—a moral geography of compassion.

Ashodhiya's poetic voice does not echo Gupt; it converses with him, extending his light into a new linguistic dawn. As Gupt humanized the divine, so Ashodhiya universalizes that humanity.

"Where Duty became Love, and Love became Dharma."

That is both the motto of this book and the essence of its achievement.

Citation Information

Recommended Academic Citation (MLA style):

Ashodhiya, Anand Kumar. SĀKET — *An English Transcreation: Inspired by the Hindi Epic Sākēt of Maithili Sharan Gupt*. Avikavani Publishers, 2025.

Review Author: Dr. Babu Ram (D.Litt.)
Professor and Chairperson, Department of Hindi,
Baba Mast Nath University, Rohtak, Haryana

Prepared for inclusion in *Critical Review Appendix*, Avikavani Publishers, 2025.

From the Transcreator's Journal — "Every act of remembrance is a new creation."

APPENDIX II Selected Hindi Stanzas from Maithili Sharan Gupt's Sākēt

(Devanāgarī Text – Representative Passages)

राम तुम्हारा वृत्त स्वयं ही काव्य है,
कोई कवि बन जाय, सहज सम्भाव्य है।

Rāma, Thy life itself is poetry;
whoever becomes a poet finds it
inevitable in Thee.

— *Sākēt*, Pratham Sarga, Verse 1

अयि दयामयि देवि, सुखदे, सारदे,
इधर भी निज वरद-पाणि पसार दे।

O Compassionate Goddess, O Giver of
Joy, O Śāradā,
extend Thy blessing-hand even unto
me.

— *Pratham Sarga*, Invocation

धरा पर धर्मादर्श-निकेत,
धन्य है स्व-सदृश साकेत।

Upon the earth stands the shrine of Dharma,
blessed is Ayodhya, mirror of heaven.

स्वर्ग की तुलना उचित ही है यहाँ,
किन्तु सुरसरिता कहाँ, सरयू कहाँ?

Fair is the heaven's likeness here—
yet where is Ganga's grace, where is Sarayū's soul?

और वह लोकेश लीला-धाम है,
भक्त-वत्सलता इसी का नाम है।

And that divine abode of deeds—
there, compassion to devotees is the true name of love.

सर्वदा स्वच्छन्द छज्जों के तले,
प्रेम के आदर्श पारावत पले।

Beneath each eave of freedom dwell
the doves of love, eternal and serene.

"धन्य है प्यारी, तुम्हारी योग्यता,
मोहिनी-सी मूर्ति, मंजु-मनोज्ञता।"

"Blessed art thou, beloved, in thy
grace—
an image of charm, a melody of
tenderness."

और सीता के समान सहनशीलता,
यही साकेत की महिमा है।

And Sītā's endurance—
the quiet glory of Sākēt forevermore.

(Editor's Note: The above verses are selected for their lyrical, ethical, and devotional essence. They preserve Gupt's original chhand and diction, forming a textual bridge for English readers and scholars.)

APPENDIX III
Glossary of Sanskrit and Cultural Terms

Term	Transliteration / Meaning	Context in Sākēt
धर्म (Dharma)	Righteousness, cosmic and moral order	Central ideal governing the conduct of Rāma, Sītā, and Ayodhyā
साकेत (Sākēt)	Ancient poetic name of Ayodhya; "The City of Dharma"	Title of Gupt's Mahākāvya; symbol of spiritual harmony
वनवास (Vanavāsa)	Exile to the forest	The period of trial for Rāma, Sītā, and Lakṣmaṇa

अग्नि-परीक्षा (Agni-Parīkṣā)	Trial by Fire	Sītā's ordeal symbolizing purity and societal judgment
भक्ति (Bhakti)	Devotional love and surrender	Embodied by Shabarī and Hanumān
कर्म (Karma)	Deed, moral action and consequence	Root of human destiny in Gupt's moral cosmos
सीता (Sītā)	The feminine ideal of purity, endurance, and truth	Symbol of the soul tested by sorrow
राम-राज्य (Rāma-Rājya)	The reign of Dharma and justice	The utopian moral order at the end of the poem
शक्ति (Śakti)	The divine feminine power	Manifested through Sītā and the

		spiritual Mother
भ्रातृ-भक्ति (Bhrātr-Bhakti)	Brotherly devotion	Lakṣmaṇa's loyalty and Urmilā's silent strength

(Editorial Note: All Sanskrit diacritics follow IAST conventions. Definitions combine textual, philosophical, and contextual meanings.)

APPENDIX IV
GLOSSARIAL NOTES AND COMMENTARY

(Select Terms from the World of Sākēt)

Ātman (आत्मन्)

The self or soul — not the ego, but the inner witness. In Gupt's vision, the journey of Rama and Sita is the awakening of the Ātman through action and surrender. Every exile, therefore, becomes a return to the Self.

Bhakti (भक्ति)

Devotion — the soul's direct communion with the Divine. In *Sākēt*, bhakti is not emotion alone but disciplined tenderness: the moral emotion of service. Love becomes sacred when illumined by duty.

Dharma (धर्म)

The eternal law of righteousness that governs both cosmos and conscience. For Gupt, *dharma* is not dogma but balance — the harmony between justice and compassion, renunciation and engagement.

Maryādā (मर्यादा)

The moral boundary that ennobles freedom. Rama, called *Maryādā–Purushottama*, embodies the dignity of restraint — the strength that chooses the right, even against desire.

Sākēt (साकेत)

The eternal city of the soul — symbolic Ayodhya. In spiritual allegory, *Sākēt* represents the inner harmony where duty becomes love and love becomes dharma. It is less a place than a realization.

Rāma (राम)

The human manifestation of divinity. In Gupt's poetic theology, Rāma is not remote Godhead but moral exemplar — divinity expressed through human virtue and disciplined compassion.

Sītā (सीता)

The feminine radiance of truth and endurance. Gupt's Sītā transforms suffering into grace; her silence is moral eloquence, her exile — the purification of the world's conscience.

Rāma–Rājya (रामराज्य)

The reign of moral order, the civilization of justice and empathy. In *Sākēt*, this is not political utopia but ethical realization — when each heart becomes Ayodhya, governed by conscience and compassion.

Tapa (तप)

Spiritual austerity — not self–denial, but inner concentration of energy. The forest hermitages in *Sākēt* are symbols of tapasya: where renunciation becomes luminous self-control.

Yajña (यज्ञ)

The sacred act of offering — not merely ritual fire, but the inner sacrifice of ego. In Gupt's verse, every act of duty becomes yajña: when one's life itself becomes an offering to the divine order.

Guru (गुरु)

The spiritual guide — the awakener of remembrance. The figure of Jatāyu, and later Shabari, both function as *gurus* in *Sākēt*: messengers who remind humanity of the eternal law of love.

Samsāra (संसार)

The world-process — the cyclic journey through birth and death. For Gupt, samsāra is not illusion but education: the field where the soul learns compassion through consequence.

Mokṣa (मोक्ष)

Liberation — the stillness attained when duty and love merge. In *Sākēt*, mokṣa is realized not by withdrawal, but through the perfected practice of dharma in worldly life.

Rāvaṇa (रावण)

The shadow of intellect without compassion. Gupt portrays Rāvaṇa not as sheer evil but as tragic grandeur — a fallen sage who mirrors the human intellect estranged from humility.

Sahṛdaya (सहृदय)

The "like-hearted" reader — one whose heart resonates with the poet's emotion. Gupt's moral universe assumes the *sahṛdaya* reader as participant, not spectator, in the drama of dharma.

Śraddhā (श्रद्धा)

Faith — not belief without reason, but trust born of experience. The devotion of Shabari and the loyalty of Hanuman manifest *śraddhā* as action guided by love.

Manava–Dharma (मानव धर्म)

The human dimension of righteousness. Gupt's highest insight is that divinity itself fulfills humanity: Rāma is God because he is perfectly human.

Anugraha (अनुग्रह)

Grace — the silent blessing that flows when effort and surrender meet. In *Sākēt*, grace is the invisible bridge between man's striving and divine compassion.

Bhāva (भाव)

The inner emotion that gives life to poetic form. To Gupt, *bhāva* is the true soul of poetry — the moral emotion of harmony where feeling becomes understanding.

———

(This glossary draws upon Sanskrit poetics, Gupt's own usage, and the transcreator's interpretive commentary to aid modern readers of the English transcreation of Sākēt.)

APPENDIX V
Chronology of Maithili Sharan Gupt (1886–1964)

Year	Event / Publication	Significance
1886	Born in Chirgaon, Jhansi (U.P.)	Birth of one of modern Hindi's earliest epic poets
1909	Publication of *Rang Mein Bhang*	Early satirical collection, social awakening
1910	*Jayadrath-Vadh*	First major work in Hindi kharī bolī poetry

1911–12	*Bharat-Bharati*	Nationalist epic — celebrated during the freedom movement
1931–32	*Sākēt* published by Lokbhārati / Jñānpīṭh (later ed.)	Spiritual epic centered on Sītā; hailed as Gupt's magnum opus
1932–40	Works like *Panchavati*, *Yashodhara*, *Dwāpār*	Continued exploration of moral dharma and gendered devotion
1947	Independence of India	Gupt honored as *Rāṣṭra-Kavi* (National Poet)
1952	Nominated to Rajya Sabha	Recognition of cultural leadership

1964	Passed away in Jhansi	Legacy continued through academic study and translations

Editorial Commentary

Gupt's *Sākēt* stands as a bridge between *Vālmīki's Rāmāyaṇa* and the modern humanist vision of India's renaissance poets. His mastery of kharī bolī Hindi elevated the language to the dignity of epic verse. By reimagining Ayodhya not as divine geography but as moral geography, he forged a timeless mirror for civilization itself.

APPENDIX VI
Bibliography & Critical References

Primary Sources (Hindi Editions of *Sākēt*)

1. **Gupt, Maithili Sharan.** *Sākēt.*
   Allahabad: Lokbhārati Prakashan, 1956 (Reprint 1980). Critical annotated Hindi edition.

2. **Gupt, Maithili Sharan.** *Sākēt* (Text with Commentary).
   Gorakhpur: Gita Press, 1963. Authorized devotional edition.

3. **Gupt, Maithili Sharan.** *Kāvy-Sanchayan (Vol. II).*
   New Delhi: Sahitya Akademi, 1985. Scholarly compilation with biographical notes.

4. *Sākēt* (Digital Archive PDF).
   Internet Archive Identifier: *2015.241745.Saket_text.pdf* (Public Domain, India, 2015).

Critical and Biographical Studies

1. **Dwivedi, Hazari Prasad.** *Hindi Sāhitya kā Itihās*. Delhi: Rajkamal Prakashan, 1952.
   – Insight into Gupt's role in Hindi literary nationalism.

2. **Singh, Ram Vilas.** *Ādhunik Hindi Kāvya ke Mūl Pravāh*. Allahabad: Kitab Mahal, 1972.
   – Contextual study of *Sākēt* as a moral-epic in the modern bhāṣā tradition.

3. **Nand Dulare Vajpayee.** *Kāvyānanda aur Gupt-ji*. Allahabad: Hindi Sahitya Sammelan, 1958.
   – Detailed stylistic and philosophical critique of Gupt's verse.

4. **Pandey, Ganga Sahay.** *Mahākavi Maithili Sharan Gupt: Vyaktitva aur Kṛtitva*. Varanasi: Chowkhamba, 1968.
   – Biographical and cultural study emphasizing Gupt's reformist dharma.

5. **Raghukul Tilak (ed.).** *Gupt-Racanāvali*. Delhi: Bharatiya Sahitya Parishad, 1974.
   – Collected works, with authentic text

variants of *Sākēt* and *Jayadrath Vadh.*

6. **Pande, Ramesh Chandra.** *Hindi Epic Tradition: From Bhāsa to Gupt.* Delhi: Motilal Banarsidass, 1999.
   – Comparative exploration of Indian and Western epic conventions.

Comparative & Theoretical Works

1. **Milton, John.** *Paradise Lost.* Ed. Alastair Fowler. London: Longman, 1998.

2. **Tagore, Rabindranath.** *Gītāñjali.* London: Macmillan, 1913.

3. **Tennyson, Alfred Lord.** *Idylls of the King.* London: Macmillan, 1885.

4. **Eliot, T. S.** *The Sacred Wood.* London: Methuen, 1920.
   – On tradition and the poetic conscience.

5. **Radhakrishnan, S.** *Indian Philosophy.* Vol. II. London: George Allen & Unwin, 1927.
   – Philosophical context of dharma and consciousness in Indian epics.

APPENDIX VII

Index of Names & Concepts

A

Agni-Pariksha – The trial of purity undergone by Sita; symbolizes moral illumination.
Ayodhya – The sacred city of Rama; represents ideal polity and inner dharma.

B

Bhakti – Devotional surrender; emotional essence of Gupt's poetry.
Bharata – Younger brother of Rama; the emblem of renunciation and fidelity.

D

Dharma – The eternal law of righteousness; recurring axis of *Sākēt*.
Dasharatha – King of Ayodhya; tragic father torn between love and duty.

G

Gupt, Maithili Sharan (1886–1964) – National poet of India; pioneer of modern Hindi epic form.

H

Hanuman – The ideal sevak; messenger of love and faith.

K

Kaikeyi – Queen of Ayodhya whose moral confusion triggers the exile.

Karma – Action bound with moral consequence; philosophical undercurrent of the poem.

L

Lakshmana – Brother of Rama; embodies service and silent heroism.

M

Maithili – Another name for Sita; also, Gupt's devotional muse.

Manthara – The maid whose jealousy sets the wheel of destiny in motion.

R

Rama – Hero of *Sākēt*; divine yet human exemplar of righteousness.

Ravana – The antagonist; embodiment of ego subdued by dharma.

S

Sākēt – Poetic name for Ayodhya; literal meaning "abode of peace."

Sita – The soul of *Sākēt*; archetype of feminine strength and purity.

Sugriva – Ally of Rama; symbolizes the strength of fellowship.
Shabari – Devotee of Rama; epitome of faith untainted by ritualism.

V
Valmiki – The seer-poet; represents the creative conscience of dharma.
Vanavāsa – Exile in forest; spiritual crucible of transformation.

APPENDIX VIII Institutional Credits/ Acknowledgments

This English *transcreation* of *Sākēt* owes its inspiration to the timeless voice of **Mahākavi Maithili Sharan Gupt**, whose humanistic dharma still guides the spirit of Hindi literature.
The transcreator extends gratitude to:

- **Lokbhārati Prakashan**, Allahabad, for preserving the authentic text.

- **Gita Press**, Gorakhpur, for its devotional edition of *Sākēt*.

- **Sahitya Akademi**, New Delhi, for their scholarly compilations.

- **Internet Archive (India Office Collection)** for the public-domain digital text.

- **Libraries and mentors** who sustained the vision of this bilingual project.

- And above all, the **readers**, who continue to believe that poetry is not mere ornament, but a **moral light**.

"May every reader who enters Sākēt find peace in Dharma and delight in verse."

From the Transcreator's Journal

— **Anand Kumar Ashodhiya**
Transcreator of SĀKET
Avikavani Publishers, 2025

Personal Acknowledgments

This work, *Sākēt: An English Devotional Epic*, is not merely a literary endeavour but a spiritual homage — a gesture of cultural devotion to the immortal tradition of Dharma and the poetic legacy of Maithili Sharan Gupt. It is the fruit of years of creative meditation, disciplined labour, and an unbroken faith in the power of language to heal and elevate the human spirit.

The journey of bringing the depth of *Rāma, Sītā,* and the moral universe of *Ayodhyā* into the rhythms of English verse has never been a solitary act. It has been guided, strengthened, and sanctified by the blessings of mentors, the affection of family, and the generous faith of many companions along the way.

My heart bows in gratitude before all those pillars of strength whose invisible hands helped shape this offering of words.

I. Family: The Foundation of Love and Endurance

My deepest thanks to my wife, **Mrs. Pushpa Anand Ashodhiya**, whose quiet patience and understanding have been the calm background of every creative dawn. Her silent strength nurtured the stillness required for such work.

To my children — **Vipin Anand Ashodhiya**, **Pooja Anand**, and **Preeti Ashodhiya**, and to my beloved granddaughters **Avani** and **Avika** — I owe a lifetime of affection. You all accepted my hours of solitude as part of a larger dream. This book is as much a tribute to your forbearance as to my faith.

II. Guru and Lineage

I remain forever indebted to my revered *Gurudev*, **Late Shri Paleram Dahiya Halalpuriya**, from whom I learned the dignity of the stage, the warmth of the word, and the living soul of metre and song. This work is humbly dedicated to his memory and his unending inspiration.

III. Friends, Critics, and Fellow Travellers

This book could not have reached its form without the discerning eyes and generous hearts of my literary companions — **Shri Ashok Kumar (Dhana, Jhajjar), Dr. Chandra Dutt Sharma (Rohtak), Kavi Dinesh Sharma, Smt. Saroj Dahiya, Smt. Vyanjana Anand (Divyalaya – Ek Sahityik Yatra),** and **Shri Rambeer Singh, Principal, Brahmashakti School, Thana Kala.** Your dialogue, critique, and encouragement turned effort into excellence.

V. Readers and Seekers

Finally, to my readers — known and unseen — who will walk with this poem through time, I offer my silent thanks. If I have written the words, you have breathed life into them. Where gratitude exists, creation ceases to be merely art — it becomes relationship.

— **Anand Kumar Ashodhiya**
Transcreator of SĀKET
Avikavani Publishers, 2025

APPENDIX IX
Author Biography

Anand Kumar Ashodhiya
(Poet, Writer, and Cultural Representative)

Anand Kumar Ashodhiya — known in the Haryanvi literary world by his pen name *Kavi Anand Shahpur* — embodies a rare confluence of creativity, discipline, and the living pulse of folk tradition. A former Warrant Officer of the Indian Air Force, he served the nation for thirty-two years, carrying into his literary work the same clarity, order, and inner strength that defined his service.

A postgraduate in English Literature from Annamalai University, Ashodhiya has always remained rooted in the resonant soil of Hindi and Haryanvi culture. His poetic name "Anand Shahpur" honours his ancestral village Shahpur Turk (District Sonipat, Haryana) and continues the musical legacy of his mentor, the legendary folk poet Paleram Dahiya Halalpuriya.

As a **custodian of Haryanvi folk heritage**, he is not only a composer of *Ragini* (folk ballads) but also a scholar of its *pingal* (prosody) and performative tradition. His works unite the lyricism of folklore with the reflective spirit of modern poetics.

Born on **1 April** in Shahpur Turk, Haryana, to Shri Raghbir Singh and Smt. Ratni Devi, he now resides in Mumbai. His life unites two poles — the discipline of a soldier and the imagination of a poet. Decorated for his contribution to *Rajbhasha Hindi* in the Air Force for eight consecutive years, he has been writing prolifically since his retirement in 2016.

He has authored over **250 compositions** across genres — *dohā, geet, ghazal, short story, and especially Haryanvi folk poetry*. His celebrated works include *Adhirājan* (folk epic in Ragini form), *Thara Mudda Thari Baat*, *Kissa Bhagat Puranmal*, *Heer Ranjha*, *Avikāvani*, *Draupadi: A Folk Consciousness*, and *Prem ke Sau Rang*. His dramas and poetic performances on YouTube have also gained wide appreciation.

A recipient of numerous cultural honours — including *Haryana Sanskriti Gaurav Ratna, Kargil Vijay Samman, Paramveer Samman,* and *Haryanvi Sahitya Ratna 2025* — he remains devoted to the preservation of India's living oral traditions.

For Anand Kumar Ashodhiya, literature is not merely art — it is *a cultural vow, a spiritual discipline, and a bridge between heritage and humanity*. Through his writing, he seeks to carry the voice of India's folk culture to the national and global stage, and to enrich modern Hindi literature with clarity, compassion, and faith.

From the Transcreator's Vision

> "My pen stands at the meeting of
> Dharma and folk memory.
> The language may change — the soul
> remains the same."

SHORT ABSTRACT FOR JACKET / PRESS RELEASE

***SĀKET*: An English Devotional Epic** reimagines Maithili Sharan Gupt's Hindi classic *Sākēt* for the modern reader. Written in luminous blank verse, Anand Kumar Ashodhiya's transcreation unites the moral radiance of ancient Ayodhya with the reflective voice of modern spirituality. Across eight poetic cantos — from exile to return, from sorrow to illumination — this work celebrates not mythology but the living rhythm of human dharma. Bridging Milton's grandeur and Tagore's compassion, *Sākēt* emerges as a universal epic of love, duty, and divine remembrance.

AUTHOR PHOTOGRAPH AND CAPTION

Anand Kumar Ashodhiya
Poet • Author • Cultural Envoy

A former Warrant Officer of the Indian Air Force with 32 years of distinguished service, Anand Kumar Ashodhiya combines the discipline of a soldier with the sensitivity of a poet. Known in Haryana's literary world as *Kavi Anand Shahpur*, he has written extensively in Hindi and Haryanvi on themes of valor, devotion, and cultural heritage. His literary imprint *Avikavani Publishers* is dedicated to preserving India's folk and classical traditions through modern expression. He lives in Mumbai, India.

COLOPHON

Title: *SĀKET: An English Transcreation*
Original Hindi Source: *Sākēt* by *Maithili Sharan Gupt* — Public Domain, India
English Transcreation: © *Anand Kumar Ashodhiya, 2025*
Imprint: *Avikavani Publishers*
Edition: First Edition, 2025
Design & Layout: Avikavani Publishers

TABLE OF CONTENTS